Chocolate Truffles

Dedication

To my wonderful children, Basile and Eloise.
—Elisabeth Antoine

To my wonderful husband, Rich, and
my two darling daughters, Olivia and Isabelle.
—Elizabeth Cunningham Herring

Acknowledgments

*We would like to thank our families and friends for their support and
patience with us as we experimented with different recipes.*

*We would especially like to thank Julia Erickson and Julie Pauly and
The Able Baker crew for all their help and support.*

*We would also like to thank our agent, Coleen O'Shea, and our publisher,
Robin Haywood.*

Published by Sellers Publishing, Inc.
Text and photography copyright © 2012 Elisabeth Antoine & Elizabeth Cunningham Herring
All rights reserved.

Sellers Publishing, Inc.
161 John Roberts Road, South Portland, Maine 04106
Visit our Web site: www.sellerspublishing.com
E-mail: rsp@rsvp.com

ISBN 13: 978-1-4162-0696-5
e-ISBN: 978-1-4162-0864-8
Library of Congress Control Number: 2012931587

Chocolate Truffles

Yummy, Sweet, Irresistible

Text and Photography by

ELISABETH ANTOINE and ELIZABETH CUNNINGHAM HERRING

SELLERS
PUBLISHING

Contents

White Chocolate Truffles

Truffle-Inspired Desserts

Marzipan Dark Chocolate Truffles, page 47

Introduction

A small ball of rich, velvety chocolate, the truffle is the very essence of decadent pleasure.

The first chocolate truffle was actually a mistake. Legend has it that in the 1920s an apprentice to famed French chef Auguste Escoffier accidentally spilled hot cream into a bowl of chopped chocolate, which when hardened was transformed into ganache, a dense, rich chocolate. It was indeed a very happy accident.

When rolled into a small ball and coated in cocoa, the ganache bore a strong resemblance to truffles, the rare and costly mushrooms found by foraging pigs in the Perigord region in France. And so the couture chocolate candy was christened. It remains today almost as celebrated as its namesake.

Though expensive to buy, the chocolate truffle is one of the simplest desserts to make at home. And it lends itself to all sorts of creative interpretations. Adding nuts or spices, liqueurs or fruits enhances the chocolate and transforms these little balls into extraordinary confections.

In this book we've included a detailed step-by-step guide to making truffles as well as dipping, rolling, and decorating them. This is followed by four sections: the first focuses on dark chocolate recipes, the second on milk chocolate, the third on white chocolate, and the last on elegant truffle-inspired desserts.

Truffles make exquisite gifts, a little treasure unwrapped with pleasure by the recipient. With this in mind, we've included a guide to packaging and presenting these delectable bite-sized morsels.

With this book, some good-quality chocolate (the better the quality, the better the results), and heavy cream, in no time you will be a master chocolatier, impressing and delighting your friends with an array of delicious, enticing truffles!

Materials and Techniques

How to Make Truffles

It's hard to believe that truffles — so elegant and sophisticated — can be so easy to make. Just follow the simple step-by-step instructions on the following pages and you will be rewarded with a trove of tasty truffles.

Get your equipment ready. For the basic dark truffle recipe, you will need the following materials: small saucepan, wooden spoon, sharp knife, medium bowl, measuring cups, measuring spoons, parchment paper (or plastic wrap).

Chop chocolate so
it is fine.

Place chopped chocolate
in the bowl.

4.

Pour heavy cream in the saucepan.

5.

Place the saucepan on the stove over medium heat.

6.

Bring the cream just to a simmer.

7.

Pour the cream over the chocolate.

8.

Wait 1 minute.

9.

Mix the cream and chocolate with a wooden spoon vigorously until all the chocolate is melted.

10.

The mixture should be smooth. If not all the chocolate is melted, see Truffle Tips on page 17 for further instructions.

11.

Add vanilla extract and stir until it is fully incorporated.

Let ganache cool at room temperature for 30 minutes. You may want to then transfer the ganache to a clean bowl.

Cut parchment paper to fit the top of the truffle mix and place the paper on the surface of the ganache. Place the bowl in the refrigerator for about 2 hours. You may also use plastic wrap to cover the ganache.

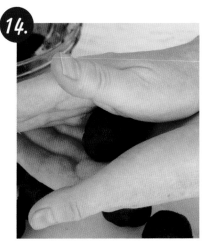

14.

Take walnut-sized spoonfuls of ganache and roll in your hands. The truffles don't have to look perfect at this point.

15.

Place the balls on parchment paper and return to the refrigerator for about an hour more.

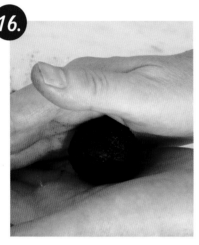

16.

Roll the ganache again to desired level of perfection. (If you plan to dip the ganache in chocolate, you may want them to be smoother and more perfectly formed than if you plan to roll them in cocoa or nuts.)

17.

Immediately after re-rolling each truffle, roll it in pure cocoa powder. Do not delay or the coating will not stick to the truffle.

18.

Place in a parchment-lined resealable container and store at room temperature for up to 4 days or in the refrigerator for up to a week. Make sure to bring them to room temperature before serving.

Truffle Tips

- If chocolate is not fully melted, you can place the bowl over a pot of hot water and stir chocolate until it finishes melting.
- If the fat in the chocolate starts to separate, you can fix it by stirring more vigorously or you can use an immersion blender to smooth it out.
- If the ganache is too hard to work with, let it sit out at room temperature for a while.
- If the ganache is too soft to work with, place it in the refrigerator or freezer for a few minutes until it firms up.
- If the outer chocolate coating gets spotted or streaked, the chocolate was not correctly tempered.
- If the outer chocolate coating cracks, the ganache was too cold when it was dipped.

Coating Your Truffles

The easiest method is to roll them in cocoa powder or another dry topping.

When the truffle is freshly formed into a ball, roll it in your favorite coating. Shown below are some popular ones: cocoa powder, confectioners' sugar, chopped nuts, coconut, and ground amaretto cookies. If you find that the ganache has become too hard and the coatings won't stick, roll the ganache ball in your hands for a moment to warm it up and soften the exterior.

Rolling truffles results in a more organic-looking truffle. These are a little messier than the dipped truffles. You may want to store them separately from truffles with different coatings as they may rub off on each other.

Dipping Truffles

Dipping the truffles in chocolate requires a bit more time, but the results are well worth it. Glossy and smooth, dipped truffles are able to accommodate lovely decorations.

To start you will need either tempered chocolate (see page 27) or chocolate coating (see page 28).

Here are two methods for dipping truffles.

Get your equipment ready. Shown here are a medium heatproof bowl, dipping tools, foam board, short skewers, parchment paper, cutting board, sharp knife, serving plate for finished truffles.

2.

After you have tempered your chocolate (see page 27), place it in the bowl. Place a truffle on the circular tool or fork and carefully dip it in the chocolate, making sure to cover it completely.

3.

Gently scrape the excess chocolate from the bottom of the truffle on the edge of the bowl.

4.

Carefully place the truffle on parchment paper to dry.

5.

You can also use the "lollipop" method. Spear a truffle with a short skewer.

6.

Dip the truffle in the chocolate.

7.

Allow the excess chocolate to drip off by tapping the skewer gently against the side of the bowl.

8.

Insert the skewer with the truffle "lollipop" in the foam board to dry.

9.

If you want to add a decoration, place it on the truffle before the coating dries.

10.

Carefully cut off any excess chocolate that may have formed on the bottom of the truffle when it was drying.

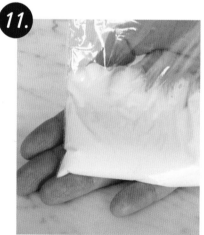

11.

If you would like to add a drizzle, place another type of melted chocolate in a resealable plastic bag.

12.

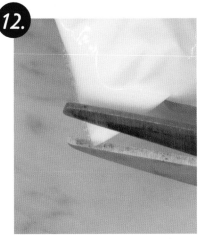

Snip off a tiny corner of the bag as shown.

13.

Carefully drizzle the chocolate over the truffles in any pattern you choose. Make sure the coating is dry before you drizzle on it.

14.

And you have a tray of elegant truffles.

How to Temper Chocolate

In order to achieve a smooth glossy finish, you will need to temper your chocolate before you dip the truffles in it. The easiest way to do this is to seed the chocolate.

Make sure to use quality chocolate with a high cocoa butter content, often labeled couverture chocolate. Chop the chocolate finely and place about half of it in a bain marie (or a heatproof bowl over a saucepan of simmering water). Stir every so often until the chocolate is fully melted. Check the temperature. For dark chocolate, it should be 115°F (46°C); for milk and white chocolate, it should read 110°F (43°C). Remove the bowl from the saucepan and place it on a dishtowel.

Now it is time to seed. Start adding the rest of the chocolate a little at a time, stirring it vigorously. When it has been added, check the temperature again. For dark it should be 90°F (32°C) and for milk and white it should be 88°F (31°C). It should have a shiny appearance. If it is not the right temperature, you can rewarm it over the saucepan.

To test the chocolate, dip a metal spoon in it and then place the spoon in the refrigerator for a few minutes. If the chocolate looks glossy and firm when you take it out, it is good to go. If it's streaky or spotty, something went wrong in the process and you'll have to start over.

You may want to place the bowl on a heating pad set on low to sustain the temperature while you are dipping your truffles.

Another Option: Using Chocolate Coating

With patience, anyone can temper chocolate. However, tempering can be a bit challenging due to the fickle nature of chocolate. If you feel daunted by the prospect, fear not. There is an easier way, though you may have to sacrifice a little flavor.

Chocolate coating is widely available in supermarkets and craft stores and on the Internet. It's easy to use and, more importantly, absolutely foolproof. Chocolate coating usually comes with instructions, but most brands call for you to microwave the chocolate in a bowl for 30-second intervals at 30 percent power until it is melted and smooth. You'll find that the truffles dipped in chocolate coating dry much faster than those dipped in the tempered chocolate. They will also look perfect. However, the taste will not be as rich and chocolaty.

Dark Chocolate Truffles

Classic Dark Chocolate Truffles

These are classics. To ensure the richest, most velvety flavor, make sure to use the best-quality chocolate you can find. We rolled these in cocoa powder, but you can also roll them in chopped nuts or dip them in dark chocolate or anything else you can think of. The possibilities are endless. **Makes about 30 truffles.**

16 ounces dark semisweet
chocolate, finely chopped
1 cup heavy cream

1 teaspoon vanilla extract
3/4 cup unsweetened cocoa powder

Instructions:

Place chopped chocolate in a medium bowl. Place cream in a saucepan and heat over a medium setting until it is just simmering. Remove the cream from the heat and pour it over the chocolate. Let it sit for a minute and then stir vigorously until all the chocolate is melted. When the mixture is smooth, add the vanilla and stir until it is fully incorporated.

Let the ganache cool at room temperature for 30 minutes. Cover the top of the ganache with plastic wrap or parchment cut to fit (the wrap or parchment should sit gently on top of the ganache). Place the bowl in the refrigerator until the ganache is firm (for about 2 hours).

When it is set, scoop out a little more than a teaspoon of the ganache and roll it between the palms of your hands to form a 3/4-inch or walnut-sized ball. The truffles don't have to look perfect at this point. Place the balls on parchment paper and return to the refrigerator for about an hour more.

Place the cocoa powder in a medium bowl. Take the truffles out of the refrigerator and roll each ball again until it is smooth and round and then immediately roll it in the cocoa powder until it is evenly coated. Continue rolling until all the truffles are covered and place them in a single layer in a parchment-lined resealable container.

For best flavor, store truffles at room temperature for up to 4 days or in the refrigerator for up to a week. If you do store them in the refrigerator, make sure to bring the truffles to room temperature before serving.

These apricot almond truffles are a bit more substantial than most, offering a heart-healthy dose of dried fruit and nuts to your dark chocolate. To make this decadent diet complete, pair it with a glass of red wine. **Makes about 30 truffles.**

8 dried apricots, very finely chopped

2 tablespoons Grand Marnier
  or Cointreau

18 ounces bittersweet chocolate,
  finely chopped

1 cup heavy cream

¼ teaspoon almond extract

1 cup raw almonds, finely chopped

Instructions:

Place the finely chopped dried apricots in a bowl with the Grand Marnier or Cointreau. Set aside.

Place chopped bittersweet chocolate in a medium bowl. Place cream in a saucepan and heat over a medium setting until it is just coming to a simmer. Remove the cream from the heat and pour it over the chocolate. Let it sit for a minute.

Stir the chocolate/cream mixture vigorously until all the chocolate is melted and the mixture is smooth. Add the almond extract and then stir in the apricot mixture until well blended.

Let the ganache cool at room temperature for 30 minutes. Cover the top of the ganache with plastic wrap or parchment cut to fit (the wrap or parchment should sit gently on top of the ganache). Place the bowl in the refrigerator until the ganache is firm (for about 2 hours).

When it is set, scoop out a little more than a teaspoon of the ganache and roll between the palms of your hands to form a ¾-inch or walnut-sized ball. The truffles don't have to look perfect at this point. Place the balls on parchment paper and return to the refrigerator for about an hour more.

Place the chopped almonds in a medium bowl. Take the truffles out of the refrigerator and roll each ball again until it is smooth and round and then immediately roll it in the chopped almonds until it is evenly coated. Continue rolling until all the truffles are covered and place them in a single layer in a parchment-lined resealable container.

For best flavor, store truffles at room temperature for up to 4 days or in the refrigerator for up to a week. If you do store them in the refrigerator, make sure to bring the truffles to room temperature before serving.

Espresso Amaretto Dark Chocolate Truffles

We've distilled the flavors of this traditional after-dinner favorite into a sophisticated bite-sized dessert. Rolling the truffles in finely crushed amaretto cookies highlights the almond flavor inside.

Makes about 30 truffles.

4 tablespoons Amaretto Di
  Saronno liqueur
$^1/_4$ teaspoon almond extract
16 ounces bittersweet chocolate,
  finely chopped
1 cup heavy cream

2 teaspoons instant espresso powder
1 cup finely crushed amaretto
  cookies
Chocolate coffee beans for
  decoration (optional)

Instructions:

Place the amaretto and almond extract in a small bowl and set aside.

Place chopped bittersweet chocolate in a medium bowl. Place cream in a saucepan and stir in espresso powder. Heat over a medium setting until it is just coming to a simmer. Remove the cream from the heat and pour it over the chocolate. Let it sit for a minute.

Stir the chocolate/cream mixture vigorously until all the chocolate is melted and the mixture is smooth. Add the amaretto/almond mixture to the chocolate and stir until well blended.

Let the ganache cool at room temperature for 30 minutes. Cover the top of the ganache with plastic wrap or parchment cut to fit (the wrap or parchment should sit gently on top of the ganache). Place the bowl in the refrigerator until the ganache is firm (for about 2 hours).

When it is set, scoop out a little more than a teaspoon of the ganache and roll between the palms of your hands to form a $^3/_4$-inch or walnut-sized ball. The truffles don't have to look perfect at this point. Continue rolling until all the ganache is used. Place the balls on parchment paper and return to the refrigerator for about an hour more.

Place the crushed amaretto cookies in a medium bowl. Take the truffles out of the refrigerator and roll each ball again until it is smooth and round and then immediately roll it in the crushed amaretto cookies until it is evenly coated. Continue rolling until all the truffles are covered and place them in a single layer in a parchment-lined resealable container.

For best flavor, store truffles at room temperature for up to 4 days or in the refrigerator for up to a week. If you do store them in the refrigerator, make sure to bring the truffles to room temperature before serving.

Ginger Cardamom Dark Chocolate Truffles

The exotic flavorings of ginger and cardamom pair well with dark chocolate. We've rolled these truffles in finely crushed ginger snaps to further enhance their fresh, tangy flavor. **Makes about 30 truffles.**

1 tablespoon ginger juice
   (extracted from a grated piece
   of peeled ginger root)
1 teaspoon vanilla extract
1/8 teaspoon ground cardamom

16 ounces bittersweet chocolate,
   finely chopped
1 cup heavy cream
1 cup finely crushed ginger snaps

Instructions:

Grate and strain peeled ginger root to obtain 1 tablespoon of ginger juice. Place the juice in a small bowl and mix in the vanilla and cardamom. Set aside.

Place chopped bittersweet chocolate in a medium bowl. Place cream in a saucepan and heat over a medium setting until it is just coming to a simmer. Remove the cream from the heat and pour it over the chocolate. Let it sit for a minute.

Stir the chocolate/cream mixture vigorously until all the chocolate is melted and the mixture is smooth. Add the ginger/vanilla mixture to the chocolate and stir until well blended.

Let the ganache cool at room temperature for 30 minutes. Cover the top of the ganache with plastic wrap or parchment cut to fit (the wrap or parchment should sit gently on top of the ganache). Place the bowl in the refrigerator until the ganache is firm (for about 2 hours).

When it is set, scoop out a little more than a teaspoon of the ganache and roll between the palms of your hands to form a 3/4-inch or walnut-sized ball. The truffles don't have to look perfect at this point. Place the balls on parchment paper and return to the refrigerator for about an hour more.

Place the crushed ginger snaps in a medium bowl. Take the truffles out of the refrigerator and roll each ball again until it is smooth and round and then immediately roll it in the crushed ginger snaps until it is evenly coated. Continue rolling until all the truffles are covered and place them in a single layer in a parchment-lined resealable container.

For best flavor, store truffles at room temperature for up to 4 days or in the refrigerator for up to a week. If you do store them in the refrigerator, make sure to bring the truffles to room temperature before serving.

Chipotle Dark Chocolate Truffles

Chipotle has long played an integral part in traditional Mexican cuisine. Composed of finely ground jalapeño peppers that have been slowly smoked over a wood fire, the powder has a warm spicy flavor that goes particularly well with dark chocolate.   **Makes about 30 truffles.**

$^1\!/_2$ teaspoon ground cinnamon
$^1\!/_2$ teaspoon chipotle powder
1 tablespoon vanilla extract
16 ounces bittersweet chocolate,
  finely chopped

1 cup heavy cream

12 ounces dark chocolate, finely
  chopped and divided
3 ounces milk chocolate for drizzle
  (optional)

Instructions:

In a small bowl mix together the spices and vanilla extract and set aside.

Place chopped bittersweet chocolate in a medium bowl. Place cream in a saucepan and heat over a medium setting until it is just coming to a simmer. Remove the cream from the heat and pour it over the chocolate. Let it sit for a minute.

Stir the chocolate/cream mixture vigorously until all the chocolate is melted and the mixture is smooth. Add the spice/vanilla mixture to the chocolate and stir until well blended.

Let the ganache cool at room temperature for 30 minutes. Cover the top of the ganache with plastic wrap or parchment cut to fit (the wrap or parchment should sit gently on top of the ganache). Place the bowl in the refrigerator until the ganache is firm (for about 2 hours).

When it is set, scoop out a little more than a teaspoon of the ganache and roll between the palms of your hands to form a ¾-inch or walnut-sized ball. The truffles don't have to look perfect at this point. Continue rolling until all the ganache is used. Place the balls on parchment paper and return to the refrigerator for about an hour more. Roll the ganache again, smoothing out any lumps, until the balls are smooth and round. Place the truffles in a single layer in a parchment-lined resealable container.

(recipe continues on next page)

To make the outer coating, take 8 ounces of finely chopped dark chocolate and place in a bain marie (bowl over a saucepan ¼ full of water). Heat the water over medium-low heat and gently stir the chocolate as it melts. When it is completely melted, remove from the heat and stir in the remaining 4 ounces of finely chopped dark chocolate, stirring until smooth. Dip the cool ganache ball in the warm chocolate using the instructions on pages 19–23. Place on a parchment-lined pan and continue dipping until all the truffles are covered. If desired, drizzle with a little milk chocolate as shown on pages 24–25 (make sure to add the drizzle after the chocolate coating dries).

Place the truffles in a single layer in a parchment-lined sealed container.

For best flavor, store truffles at room temperature for up to 4 days or in the refrigerator for up to a week. If you do store them in the refrigerator, make sure to bring the truffles to room temperature before serving.

Many believe that the Aztecs were the first to make chipotle powder. Smoking the jalapeños and turning them into a powder would enable them to keep and store them for a much longer period of time.

Kir Royale Dark Chocolate Truffles

Based on the popular French aperitif, these truffles are a combination of crème de cassis — a delicious black currant liqueur — and dark chocolate. A splash of Champagne does little to alter the flavor, but adds to their glamour. **Makes about 24 truffles.**

(recipe continues on next page)

Kir Royale Dark Chocolate Truffles *(continued)*

16 ounces bittersweet chocolate, finely chopped
½ cup heavy cream
2 teaspoons Champagne
8 tablespoons crème de cassis, divided

12 ounces bittersweet chocolate, finely chopped and divided
Lavender sugar for decoration (optional)

Instructions:

Place 16 ounces of finely chopped bittersweet chocolate in a medium bowl. Place cream in a saucepan and stir in Champagne and 4 tablespoons of crème de cassis. Heat over a medium setting until it is just coming to a simmer. Remove the cream from the heat and pour it over the chocolate. Let it sit for a minute.

Stir the chocolate/cream mixture vigorously until all the chocolate is melted and the mixture is smooth. Add the remaining 4 tablespoons of crème de cassis to the chocolate and stir until well blended.

Let the ganache cool at room temperature for 30 minutes. Cover the top of the ganache with plastic wrap or parchment cut to fit (the wrap or parchment should sit gently on top of the ganache). Place the bowl in the refrigerator until the ganache is firm (for about 2 hours).

When it is set, scoop out a little more than a teaspoon of the ganache and roll between the palms of your hands to form a ¾-inch or walnut-sized ball. The truffles don't have to look perfect at this point. Continue rolling until all the ganache is used. Place the balls on parchment paper and return to the refrigerator for about an hour more. Roll the ganache again, smoothing out any lumps, until the balls are smooth and round.

Place the truffles in a single layer in a parchment-lined resealable container.

To make the chocolate coating, take 8 ounces of finely chopped bittersweet chocolate and place in a bain marie (bowl over a saucepan $\frac{1}{4}$ full of water). Heat the water over medium-low heat and gently stir the chocolate as it melts. When it is completely melted, remove from the heat and stir in the remaining 4 ounces of finely chopped bittersweet chocolate, stirring until smooth. Dip the cool ganache balls in the warm chocolate using the instructions on pages 19–23. Place the dipped truffles on a parchment-lined pan and, if desired, gently sprinkle some lavender sugar on the top for decoration (make sure to add the sugar before the chocolate coating dries).

Continue dipping until all the truffles are covered and decorated. Place the truffles in a single layer in a parchment-lined sealed container.

For best flavor, store truffles at room temperature for up to 4 days or in the refrigerator for up to a week. If you do store them in the refrigerator, make sure to bring the truffles to room temperature before serving.

Lavender sugar dresses up these Champagne truffles and gives them some sparkle.

Brandy Dark Chocolate Truffles

Just as brandy is a wonderful after-dinner drink, brandy truffles are a wonderful after-dinner sweet. The subtle taste of the brandy enhances the bittersweet dark chocolate, creating a luxurious indulgence. Paired with a snifter of your favorite spirit, it's a perfect finish to a sumptuous meal. **Makes about 30 truffles.**

16 ounces bittersweet chocolate, finely chopped

¾ cup heavy cream

4 teaspoons brandy (Cognac or Armagnac)

12 ounces of bittersweet chocolate, finely chopped and divided

Sugar pearls (optional)

Instructions:

Place the 16 ounces of finely chopped bittersweet chocolate in a medium bowl. Place the cream in a saucepan and heat over a medium setting until it is just coming to a simmer. Pour it over the chocolate. Let it sit for a minute.

Stir the chocolate/cream mixture vigorously until all the chocolate is melted and the mixture is smooth. Add the brandy and stir until well blended.

Let the ganache cool at room temperature for 30 minutes. Cover the top of the ganache with plastic wrap or parchment cut to fit (the wrap or parchment should sit gently on top of the ganache). Place the bowl in the refrigerator until the ganache is firm (for about 2 hours).

When it is set, scoop out a little more than a teaspoon of the ganache and roll between the palms of your hands to form a ¾-inch or walnut-sized ball. The truffles don't have to look perfect at this point. Continue rolling until all the ganache is used. Place the balls on parchment paper and return to the refrigerator for about an hour more. Roll the ganache again, smoothing out any lumps, until the balls are smooth and round.

Place the truffles in a single layer in a parchment-lined resealable container.

(recipe continues on next page)

Brandy Dark Chocolate Truffles (continued)

To make the chocolate coating, take 8 ounces of finely chopped bittersweet chocolate and place in a bain marie (bowl over a saucepan ¼ full of water). Heat the water over medium-low heat and gently stir the chocolate as it melts. When it is completely melted, remove from the heat and stir in the remaining 4 ounces of finely chopped bittersweet chocolate, stirring until smooth. Dip the cool ganache balls in the warm chocolate using the instructions on pages 19–23. Place the dipped truffles on a parchment-lined pan and, if desired, add some sugar pearls for decoration (make sure to add the pearls before the chocolate coating dries).

Continue dipping until all the truffles are covered and decorated. Place the truffles in a single layer in a parchment-lined sealed container.

For best flavor, store truffles at room temperature for up to 4 days or in the refrigerator for up to a week. If you do store them in the refrigerator, make sure to bring the truffles to room temperature before serving.

All brandies are not of equal quality. For these truffles we suggest using either Cognac or Armagnac brandies.

Marzipan Dark Chocolate Truffles

Biting into one of these dark chocolate truffles, you will discover a little surprise: a small flavorful ball of marzipan. We added a little marzipan flower for decoration as well as an extra burst of almond flavor.

Makes about 30 truffles.

(recipe continues on next page)

Marzipan Dark Chocolate Truffles (continued)

21 ounces bittersweet chocolate,
   finely chopped
2 cups heavy cream
2 teaspoons Grand Marnier
6 ounces marzipan

12 ounces bittersweet chocolate,
   finely chopped and divided
Marzipan flowers for decoration
   (optional)

Instructions:

Place 21 ounces of finely chopped bittersweet chocolate in a medium bowl. Place cream in a saucepan and heat over a medium setting until it is just coming to a simmer. Remove the cream from the heat and pour it over the chocolate. Let it sit for a minute.

Stir the chocolate/cream mixture vigorously until all the chocolate is melted and the mixture is smooth. Add the Grand Marnier to the chocolate mixture and stir until well blended.

Let the ganache cool at room temperature for 30 minutes. Cover the top of the ganache with plastic wrap or parchment cut to fit (the wrap or parchment should sit gently on top of the ganache). Place the bowl in the refrigerator until the ganache is firm (for about 2 or 3 hours).

Meanwhile, roll out marzipan paste and form small acorn-sized balls. Refrigerate on parchment paper for 30 minutes.

When the ganache is set, scoop out a little more than a teaspoon and roll between the palms of your hands to form a ¾-inch or walnut-sized ball.

Insert a marzipan ball into the center of each ganache ball. The truffles don't have to look perfect at this point. Continue rolling until all the ganache is used. Place the balls on parchment paper and return to the refrigerator for about an hour more. Roll the ganache again, smoothing out any lumps, until the balls are smooth and round.

Place the truffles in a single layer in a parchment-lined resealable container.

To make the chocolate coating, take 8 ounces of finely chopped bittersweet chocolate and place in a bain marie (bowl over a saucepan ¼ full of water). Heat the water over medium-low heat and gently stir the chocolate as it melts. When it is completely melted, remove from the heat and stir in the remaining 4 ounces of finely chopped bittersweet chocolate, stirring until smooth. Dip the cool ganache balls in the warm chocolate using the instructions on pages 19–23. Place the dipped truffles on a parchment-lined pan and, if desired, add a marzipan flower for decoration as shown on page 23 (make sure to add the decoration before the chocolate coating dries).

Continue dipping until all the truffles are covered and decorated. Place the truffles in a single layer in a parchment-lined sealed container.

For best flavor, store truffles in the refrigerator for up to a week. Make sure to bring the truffles to room temperature before serving.

You will definitely want to dip these truffles rather than roll them in a powdery coating, as the ganache is softer than that of the other dark chocolate truffles.

Butter Rum Cinnamon Dark Chocolate Truffles

Laced with cinnamon and other spices, these butter rum truffles are the epitome of adult comfort food. Like the drink of the same name, they are sure to keep you warm on a cold winter's night, or for that matter, any time at all. **Makes about 30 truffles.**

4 tablespoons dark rum
2 teaspoons dark brown sugar
2 teaspoons cinnamon
Pinch of salt
¾ cup chopped walnuts
½ cup heavy cream
½ cup unsalted butter

1 clove
1 cinnamon stick
16 ounces of bittersweet chocolate

12 ounces of bittersweet
chocolate, divided
½ teaspoon cinnamon (optional)

Instructions:

Place the rum, brown sugar, cinnamon, salt, and chopped nuts in a small bowl and set aside.

Place 16 ounces of bittersweet chocolate in a medium bowl. Place cream and butter in a saucepan and add a clove and cinnamon stick. Heat over a medium setting until it is just coming to a simmer. Remove the cream from the heat and let it sit for 10 minutes. Remove clove and cinnamon stick and return cream mixture to a simmer. Pour it over the chocolate. Let it sit for a minute.

Stir the chocolate/cream mixture vigorously until all the chocolate is melted and the mixture is smooth. Add the rum mixture and stir until well blended.

Let the ganache cool at room temperature for 30 minutes. Cover the top of the ganache with plastic wrap or parchment cut to fit (the wrap or parchment should sit gently on top of the ganache). Place the bowl in the refrigerator until the ganache is firm (for about 2 hours).

When it is set, scoop out a little more than a teaspoon of the ganache and roll between the palms of your hands to form a ¾-inch or walnut-sized ball. The truffles don't have to look perfect at this point. Continue rolling until all the ganache is used. Place the balls on parchment paper and return to the refrigerator for about an hour more. Roll the ganache again, smoothing out any lumps, until the balls are smooth and round.

(recipe continues on next page)

Place the truffles in a single layer in a parchment-lined sealed container.

To make the chocolate coating, take 8 ounces of finely chopped bittersweet chocolate and place in a bain marie (bowl over a saucepan ¼ full of water). Heat the water over medium-low heat and gently stir the chocolate as it melts. When it is completely melted, remove from the heat and stir in the remaining 4 ounces of finely chopped bittersweet chocolate, stirring until smooth. Dip the cool ganache balls in the warm chocolate using the instructions on pages 19–23. Place the dipped truffles on a parchment-lined pan and, if desired, gently sprinkle some cinnamon on the top for decoration (make sure to add the cinnamon before the chocolate coating dries).

Continue dipping until all the truffles are covered and decorated. Place the truffles in a single layer in a parchment-lined resealable container.

For best flavor, store truffles at room temperature for up to 4 days or in the refrigerator for up to a week. If you do store them in the refrigerator, make sure to bring the truffles to room temperature before serving.

The chopped walnuts were included to add some texture,
but feel free to leave them out if you prefer.

Milk Chocolate Truffles

Classic Milk Chocolate Truffles

Rich, smooth, creamy milk chocolate makes a delectable ganache that goes with many different flavors. As always, using the best-quality chocolate will yield the tastiest truffles. We've rolled these truffles in a mixture of confectioners' sugar and cocoa powder to give them a sweet chocolate coating. Of course they are also delicious rolled in nuts or dipped in chocolate. **Makes about 24 truffles.**

16 ounces milk chocolate,
   finely chopped
²⁄₃ cup heavy cream

¹⁄₂ cup confectioners' sugar
¹⁄₄ cup cocoa powder

Instructions:

Place chopped milk chocolate in a medium bowl. Place cream in a saucepan and heat over a medium setting until it is just coming to a simmer. Remove the cream from the heat and pour it over the chocolate. Let it sit for a minute and then vigorously stir until all the chocolate is melted and the mixture is smooth.

Let the ganache cool at room temperature for 30 minutes. Cover the top of the ganache with plastic wrap or parchment cut to fit (the wrap or parchment should sit gently on top of the ganache). Place the bowl in the refrigerator until the ganache is firm (for about 2 hours).

When it is set, scoop out a little more than a teaspoon of the ganache and roll between the palms of your hands to form a ¾-inch or walnut-sized ball. The truffles don't have to look perfect at this point. Continue rolling until all the ganache is used. Place the balls on parchment paper and return to the refrigerator for about an hour more.

Mix confectioners' sugar and cocoa powder in a medium bowl. Take the truffles out of the refrigerator and roll each ball again until it is smooth and round and then immediately roll it in the confectioners' sugar and cocoa powder until it is evenly coated. Continue rolling until all the truffles are covered and place them in a single layer in a parchment-lined resealable container.

For best flavor, store truffles at room temperature for up to 4 days or in the refrigerator for up to a week. If you do store them in the refrigerator, make sure to bring the truffles to room temperature before serving.

Coconut Milk Chocolate Truffles

The combination of coconut and milk chocolate has long been a favorite, one found in many popular candy bars. Here the addition of coconut cream and coconut extract intensifies the tropical coconut flavor. **Makes about 30 truffles.**

16 ounces milk chocolate, finely chopped

1/2 cup heavy cream

2 teaspoons coconut cream

1 teaspoon coconut extract

1/2 cup unsweetened coconut flakes

1 cup unsweetened coconut flakes for coating

Instructions:

Place chopped milk chocolate in a medium bowl. Place cream and coconut cream in a saucepan and heat over a medium setting until it is just coming to a simmer. Remove the cream mixture from the heat and pour it over the chocolate. Let it sit for a minute.

Stir the chocolate/cream mixture vigorously until all the chocolate is melted and the mixture is smooth. Add the coconut extract, mix well, and then add the coconut flakes and stir.

Let the ganache cool at room temperature for 30 minutes. Cover the top of the ganache with plastic wrap or parchment cut to fit (the wrap or parchment should sit gently on top of the ganache). Place the bowl in the refrigerator until the ganache is firm (for about 2 hours).

When it is set, scoop out a little more than a teaspoon of the ganache and roll between the palms of your hands to form a ¾-inch or walnut-sized ball. The truffles don't have to look perfect at this point. Place the balls on parchment paper and return to the refrigerator for about an hour more.

Place the remaining coconut flakes in a medium bowl. Take the truffles out of the refrigerator and roll each ball again until it is smooth and round and then immediately roll it in the coconut flakes until it is evenly coated. Continue rolling until all the truffles are covered and place them in a single layer in a parchment-lined resealable container.

For best flavor, store truffles at room temperature for up to 4 days or in the refrigerator for up to a week. If you do store them in the refrigerator, make sure to bring the truffles to room temperature before serving.

Peanut Butter Milk Chocolate Truffles

Any peanut butter cup fan knows that the combination of milk chocolate and peanut butter is simply irresistible. It's even better when you use fine-quality milk chocolate. For the best results, make sure to use natural peanut butter in this recipe rather than one made with hydrogenated oils. **Makes about 30 truffles.**

16 ounces milk chocolate,
  finely chopped
2/3 cup heavy cream
1 cup smooth natural peanut
  butter (not hydrogenated)

12 ounces milk chocolate, finely
  chopped and divided
1/2 cup chopped peanuts

Instructions:

Place 16 ounces of finely chopped milk chocolate in a medium bowl. Place cream in a saucepan and heat over a medium setting until it is just coming to a simmer. Remove the cream from the heat and pour it over the chocolate. Let it sit for a few minutes and then vigorously stir until it is smooth. Carefully stir in the peanut butter, making sure to mix it until it is well blended.

Let the ganache cool at room temperature for 30 minutes. Cover the top of the ganache with plastic wrap or parchment paper cut to fit (the wrap or parchment should sit gently on top of the ganache). Place the bowl in the refrigerator until the ganache is firm (for about 2 hours).

When it is set, scoop out a little more than a teaspoon of the ganache and roll between the palms of your hands to form a 3/4-inch or walnut-sized ball. Continue rolling until all the ganache is used. Place balls in a single layer on a parchment-lined cookie sheet. (You may need to put the ganache back in the refrigerator for a few minutes if it begins to get too soft.) When finished, place the pan in the refrigerator.

To make the chocolate coating, take 8 ounces of finely chopped milk chocolate and place in a bain marie (bowl over a saucepan 1/4 full of water). Heat the water over medium-low heat and gently stir the chocolate as it melts. When it is completely melted, remove from the heat and stir in the remaining 4 ounces of finely chopped milk chocolate, stirring until smooth. Dip the cool ganache balls in the warm chocolate using the instructions on pages 19–23. Place on a parchment-lined pan and, if desired, gently place chopped peanuts on the top for decoration (make sure to add the peanut topping before the chocolate coating dries).

For best flavor, store truffles in a parchment-lined resealable container at room temperature for up to 4 days or in the refrigerator for up to a week. If you do store them in the refrigerator, make sure to bring the truffles to room temperature before serving.

Orange Cardamom Milk Chocolate Truffles

With a slight citrus note, the ancient aromatic spice, cardamom, melds beautifully with both orange and milk chocolate. After dipping these truffles, we've decorated them with a bit of candied orange peel for an elegant, yet exotic finish. **Makes about 30 truffles.**

Zest of 1/2 orange
1 tablespoon vanilla extract
16 ounces milk chocolate, finely
    chopped
1 cup heavy cream
1/4 teaspoon ground cardamom

12 ounces milk chocolate, finely
    chopped and separated

Candied orange peel strips
    (optional)

Instructions:

Place the orange zest in a very small bowl with the vanilla. Set aside.

Place 16 ounces of finely chopped milk chocolate in a medium bowl. Place cream in a saucepan and heat over a medium setting until it is just coming to a simmer. Remove the cream from the heat and pour it over the chocolate. Let it sit for a minute.

In the meantime, strain the vanilla/orange zest mixture into another small bowl. Use a wooden spoon to press down on the zest to impart as much flavor as possible to the vanilla mixture. Add the ground cardamom to this mix.

Stir the chocolate/cream mixture vigorously until all the chocolate is melted and the mixture is smooth. Add the vanilla mixture to the chocolate and stir until well blended.

Let the ganache cool at room temperature for 30 minutes. Cover the top of the ganache with plastic wrap or parchment cut to fit (the wrap or parchment should sit gently on top of the ganache). Place the bowl in the refrigerator until the ganache is firm (for about 2 hours).

When it is set, scoop out a little more than a teaspoon of the ganache and roll between the palms of your hands to form a 3/4-inch or walnut-sized ball. The truffles don't have to look perfect at this point. Continue rolling until all the ganache is used. Place the balls on parchment paper and return to the refrigerator for about an hour more. Roll the ganache again, smoothing out any lumps, until the balls are smooth and round.

(recipe continues on next page)

Place the truffles in a single layer in a parchment-lined sealed container.

To make the chocolate coating, take 8 ounces of finely chopped milk chocolate and place in a bain marie (bowl over a saucepan ¼ full of water). Heat the water over medium-low heat and gently stir the chocolate as it melts. When it is completely melted, remove from the heat and stir in the remaining 4 ounces of finely chopped milk chocolate, stirring until smooth. Dip the cool ganache balls in the warm chocolate using the instructions on pages 19–23. Place the dipped truffles on a parchment-lined pan and, if desired, gently place a small piece of candied orange peel on the top for decoration (make sure to add the orange peel before the chocolate coating dries).

Continue dipping until all the truffles are covered and decorated. Place them in a single layer in a parchment-lined resealable container.

For best flavor, store truffles at room temperature for up to 4 days or in the refrigerator for up to a week. If you do store them in the refrigerator, make sure to bring the truffles to room temperature before serving.

Instead of candied orange peel, you can use a sprinkling of cardamom to decorate the top of these truffles.

Bananas Foster Milk Chocolate Truffles

It's not so surprising that Bananas Foster — a dessert combining bananas, brown sugar, and dark rum — has remained a perennial favorite since its creation in New Orleans in 1951. We've infused these classic flavors into milk chocolate ganache. The result is a yummy delight. **Makes about 30 truffles.**

(recipe continues on next page)

16 ounces milk chocolate,
  finely chopped
¼ cup heavy cream
2 tablespoons unsalted butter
2 tablespoons dark brown sugar
2 tablespoons banana puree

4 tablespoons dark rum

12 ounces milk chocolate,
  finely chopped and separated
Banana chips for decoration
  (optional)

Instructions:

Place 16 ounces of finely chopped milk chocolate in a medium bowl. Place cream, butter, sugar, and banana puree in a saucepan and heat over a medium setting until it is just coming to a simmer. Remove the cream mixture from the heat and pour it over the chocolate. Let it sit for a minute.

Stir the chocolate/cream mixture vigorously until all the chocolate is melted and the mixture is smooth. Add the rum to the chocolate and stir until well blended.

Let the ganache cool at room temperature for 30 minutes. Cover the top of the ganache with plastic wrap or parchment cut to fit (the wrap or parchment should sit gently on top of the ganache). Place the bowl in the refrigerator until the ganache is firm (for about 2 hours).

When it is set, scoop out a little more than a teaspoon of the ganache and roll between the palms of your hands to form a ¾-inch or walnut-sized ball. The truffles don't have to look perfect at this point. Continue rolling until all the ganache is used. Place the balls on parchment paper and return to the refrigerator for about an hour more. Roll the ganache again, smoothing out any lumps, until the balls are smooth and round.

Place the truffles in a single layer in a parchment-lined resealable container.

To make the chocolate coating, take 8 ounces of finely chopped milk chocolate and place in a bain marie (bowl over a saucepan $\frac{1}{4}$ full of water). Heat the water over medium-low heat and gently stir the chocolate as it melts. When it is completely melted, remove from the heat and stir in the remaining 4 ounces of finely chopped milk chocolate, stirring until smooth. Dip the cool ganache balls in the warm chocolate using the instructions on pages 19–23. Place the dipped truffles on a parchment-lined pan and, if desired, gently place a small piece of banana chip on the top for decoration (make sure to add the chip before the chocolate coating dries).

Continue dipping until all the truffles are covered and decorated. Place the truffles in a single layer in a parchment-lined resealable container.

For best flavor, store truffles in the refrigerator for up to a week. Make sure to bring the truffles to room temperature before serving.

Cinnamon is often an ingredient in Bananas Foster. If you like, you can add a teaspoon to the above recipe (to the cream mixture) for a more traditional Bananas Foster taste.

Chai Milk Chocolate Truffles

A delicious spiced milk tea from India, Chai features a delicate mix of anise, cardamom, cloves, cinnamon, pepper, and ginger. This exotic combination of spices pairs well with creamy milk chocolate.

Makes about 30 truffles.

$^1/_2$ teaspoon ground anise
$^1/_2$ teaspoon ground cardamom
$^1/_2$ teaspoon ground cloves
$^1/_2$ teaspoon ground cinnamon
$^1/_2$ teaspoon ground white pepper
16 ounces milk chocolate,
  finely chopped
$^1/_2$ cup heavy cream

2 tablespoons black tea leaves
2 tablespoons freshly grated
  ginger root

12 ounces milk chocolate, divided
3 ounces white chocolate drizzle
  for decoration (optional)

Instructions:

In a small bowl, mix together all the ground spices (anise, cardamom, cloves, cinnamon, and pepper). Set aside.

Place 16 ounces finely chopped milk chocolate in a medium bowl. Place cream in a saucepan and heat over a medium setting until it is just coming to a simmer. Remove the cream from the heat and add the tea leaves and grated ginger. Cover and let steep for 5 minutes. Strain the cream mixture and then pour the strained cream back in the pan. Bring back to a simmer. Pour it over the chocolate. Let it sit for a minute.

Stir the chocolate/cream mixture vigorously until all the chocolate is melted and the mixture is smooth. If the chocolate doesn't melt completely, put the bowl on top of a saucepan containing hot water and mix until all the chocolate is melted. (Make sure the bottom of the bowl does not touch the water.) When the mixture is smooth, add the ground spices and mix well.

Let the ganache cool at room temperature for 30 minutes. Cover the top of the ganache with plastic wrap or parchment cut to fit (the wrap or parchment should sit gently on top of the ganache). Place the bowl in the refrigerator until the ganache is firm (for about 2 hours).

(recipe continues on next page)

When it is set, scoop out a little more than a teaspoon of the ganache and roll between the palms of your hands to form a ¾-inch or walnut-sized ball. The truffles don't have to look perfect at this point. Place the balls on parchment paper and return to the refrigerator for about an hour more. Roll the ganache again, smoothing out any lumps, until the balls are smooth and round.

To make the outer coating, take 8 ounces of finely chopped milk chocolate and place in a bain marie (bowl over a saucepan ¼ full of water). Heat the water over medium-low heat and gently stir the chocolate as it melts. When it is completely melted, remove from the heat and stir in the remaining 4 ounces of finely chopped milk chocolate, stirring until smooth. Dip the cool ganache balls in the warm chocolate using the instructions on pages 19–23. Place on a parchment-lined pan. Continue dipping until all the truffles are covered. If desired, drizzle with a little white chocolate as shown on pages 24–25 (make sure to add the drizzle after the chocolate coating dries).

Place the truffles in a single layer in a parchment-lined resealable container.

For best flavor, store truffles at room temperature for up to 4 days or in the refrigerator for up to a week. If you do store them in the refrigerator, make sure to bring the truffles to room temperature before serving.

> ***Chai is the generic word for tea in many countries. The proper way to refer to the tea mixture this recipe is based on is Masala Chai, which literally means "mixed-spice tea."***

Cherry Milk Chocolate Truffles

The slightly sour flavor of cherries is a perfect foil for the sweetness of milk chocolate. To impart the deepest flavor, make sure to soak the dried cherries in the cherry liqueur for at least 30 minutes.

Makes about 30 truffles.

(recipe continues on next page)

²/₃ cup dried cherries,
   finely chopped
4 tablespoons cherry liqueur
16 ounces milk chocolate,
   finely chopped
¹/₂ cup heavy cream

¹/₂ teaspoon ground cinnamon
¹/₂ teaspoon almond extract

12 ounces milk chocolate, divided
Candied rose petals for decoration
   (optional)

Instructions:

In a small bowl, mix together the finely chopped cherries and the cherry liqueur. Let sit for about 30 minutes.

Place 16 ounces of finely chopped milk chocolate in a medium bowl. Place cream in a saucepan and heat over a medium setting until it is just coming to a simmer. Remove the cream from the heat and pour it over the chocolate. Let it sit for a minute.

Stir the chocolate/cream mixture vigorously until all the chocolate is melted and the mixture is smooth. If the chocolate doesn't melt completely, put the bowl on top of a saucepan containing hot water and mix until all the chocolate is melted. (Make sure the bottom of the bowl does not touch the water.) When the mixture is smooth, add the cherry mixture and stir gently. Add the cinnamon and almond extract and mix well.

Let the ganache cool at room temperature for 30 minutes. Cover the top of the ganache with plastic wrap or parchment cut to fit (the wrap or parchment should sit gently on top of the ganache). Place the bowl in the refrigerator until the ganache is firm (for about 2 hours).

When it is set, scoop out a little more than a teaspoon of the ganache and roll between the palms of your hands to form a ¾-inch or walnut-sized ball. The truffles don't have to look perfect at this point. Place the balls on parchment paper and return to the refrigerator for about an hour more. Roll the ganache again, smoothing out any lumps, until the balls are smooth and round.

To make the outer coating, take 8 ounces of finely chopped milk chocolate and place in a bain marie (bowl over a saucepan ¼ full of water). Heat the water over medium-low heat and gently stir the chocolate as it melts. When it is completely melted, remove from the heat and stir in the remaining 4 ounces of finely chopped milk chocolate, stirring until smooth. Dip the cool ganache balls in the warm chocolate using the instructions on pages 19–23. Place on a parchment-lined pan and, if desired, place a candied rose in the center of each truffle for decoration (make sure to add the topping before the chocolate coating dries).

Continue dipping until all the truffles are covered and decorated. Place the truffles in a single layer in a parchment-lined resealable container.

For best flavor, store truffles at room temperature for up to 4 days or in the refrigerator for up to a week. If you do store them in the refrigerator, make sure to bring the truffles to room temperature before serving.

We've topped these cherry truffles with candied rose petals, which can be found in specialty food stores or ordered online.

Hazelnut Milk Chocolate Truffles

Though ubiquitous in Europe, the combination of hazelnuts and chocolate is far less common on this side of the pond. One bite of these exquisite morsels may cause you to wonder why. To boost the flavor, we've added Frangelico hazelnut liqueur, and to enhance the crunch, we've placed a whole hazelnut in each truffle's center.

Makes about 30 truffles.

4 tablespoons Frangelico hazelnut
   liqueur
1/4 teaspoon hazelnut extract
Pinch of salt
2/3 cup toasted hazelnuts, chopped
16 ounces milk chocolate,
   finely chopped
1/4 cup heavy cream

1/4 cup unsalted butter
30 whole hazelnuts

12 ounces milk chocolate, finely
   chopped and separated
Dark chocolate curls for decoration
   (optional)

Instructions:

In a small bowl, mix together Frangelico, hazelnut extract, salt, and toasted hazelnuts. Set aside.

Place 16 ounces of finely chopped milk chocolate in a medium bowl. Place cream and butter in a saucepan and heat over a medium setting until mixture is just coming to a simmer. Remove the cream mixture from the heat and pour it over the chocolate. Let it sit for a minute.

Stir the chocolate/cream mixture vigorously until all the chocolate is melted and the mixture is smooth. Add the Frangelico mixture to the chocolate and stir until well blended.

Let the ganache cool at room temperature for 30 minutes. Cover the top of the ganache with plastic wrap or parchment cut to fit (the wrap or parchment should sit gently on top of the ganache). Place the bowl in the refrigerator until the ganache is firm (for about 2 hours).

When it is set, scoop out a little more than a teaspoon of the ganache and roll between the palms of your hands to form a 3/4-inch or walnut-sized ball. Insert a whole hazelnut into the center of the ball. The truffles don't have to look perfect at this point. Continue rolling until all the ganache is used. Place the balls on parchment paper and return to the refrigerator for about an hour more. Roll the ganache again, smoothing out any lumps, until the balls are smooth and round.

(recipe continues on next page)

Place the truffles in a single layer in a parchment-lined resealable container.

To make the chocolate coating, take 8 ounces of finely chopped milk chocolate and place in a bain marie (bowl over a saucepan ¼ full of water). Heat the water over medium-low heat and gently stir the chocolate as it melts. When it is completely melted, remove from the heat and stir in the remaining 4 ounces of finely chopped milk chocolate, stirring until smooth. Dip the cool ganache balls in the warm chocolate using the instructions on pages 19–23. Place the dipped truffles on a parchment-lined pan and, if desired, gently place a few dark chocolate curls on the top for decoration (make sure to add the curls before the chocolate coating dries).

Continue dipping until all the truffles are covered and decorated. Place the truffles in a single layer in a parchment-lined sealed container.

For best flavor, store truffles at room temperature for up to 4 days or in the refrigerator for up to a week. If you do store them in the refrigerator, make sure to bring the truffles to room temperature before serving.

Though the truffles featured here have been dipped in milk chocolate and decorated with chocolate curls, you can also roll them in chopped hazelnuts.

Hazelnuts, milk chocolate, and Frangelico are the key elements of these sinfully delicious truffles.

Bourbon Pecan Milk Chocolate Truffles

Fans of pecan pie will just love these bite-sized delights. The sweet oaky flavor of the bourbon is a perfect match for milk chocolate and crunchy toasted pecans. We chose to dip these truffles in milk chocolate and drizzled them with dark chocolate, but you can also decorate them with a whole pecan or roll them in chopped ones.

Makes about 30 truffles.

4 tablespoons bourbon
Pinch of salt
²/₃ cup toasted pecans, chopped
16 ounces milk chocolate,
    finely chopped
¹/₄ cup heavy cream

¹/₄ cup unsalted butter

12 ounces milk chocolate,
    finely chopped and separated
Dark chocolate drizzle for
    decoration (optional)

Instructions:

In a small bowl, mix together bourbon, salt, and pecans. Set aside.

Place 16 ounces of finely chopped milk chocolate in a medium bowl. Place cream and butter in a saucepan and heat over a medium setting until it is just coming to a simmer. Remove the cream mixture from the heat and pour it over the chocolate. Let it sit for a minute.

Stir the chocolate/cream mixture vigorously until all the chocolate is melted and the mixture is smooth. Add the bourbon mixture to the chocolate and stir until well blended.

Let the ganache cool at room temperature for 30 minutes. Cover the top of the ganache with plastic wrap or parchment cut to fit (the wrap or parchment should sit gently on top of the ganache). Place the bowl in the refrigerator until the ganache is firm (for about 2 hours).

When it is set, scoop out a little more than a teaspoon of the ganache and roll between the palms of your hands to form a ³/₄-inch or walnut-sized ball. The truffles don't have to look perfect at this point. Continue rolling until all the ganache is used. Place the balls on parchment paper and return to the refrigerator for about an hour more. Roll the ganache again, smoothing out any lumps, until the balls are smooth and round.

Place the truffles in a single layer in a parchment-lined sealed container.

(recipe continues on next page)

To make the chocolate coating, take 8 ounces of chopped milk chocolate and place in a bain marie (bowl over a saucepan ¼ full of water). Heat the water over medium-low heat and gently stir the chocolate as it melts. When it is completely melted, remove from the heat and stir in the remaining 4 ounces of finely chopped milk chocolate, stirring until smooth. Dip the cool ganache balls in the warm chocolate using the instructions on pages 19–23. Place the dipped truffles on a parchment-lined pan. Continue dipping until all the truffles are covered. If desired, gently drizzle dark chocolate on the top for decoration (make sure to add the drizzle after the milk chocolate coating dries).

Place the truffles in a single layer in a parchment-lined resealable container.

For best flavor, store truffles at room temperature for up to 4 days or in the refrigerator for up to a week. If you do store them in the refrigerator, make sure to bring the truffles to room temperature before serving.

Not only are pecans incredibly tasty, they are also a great source of protein.

White Chocolate Truffles

Classic White Chocolate Truffles

With its creamy texture and subtle vanilla flavorings, white chocolate is an ideal partner for a wide range of flavors, but it's also fabulous on its own. To jazz these truffles up a little bit, roll them in chopped nuts or dip them in dark chocolate. **Makes about 20 truffles.**

16 ounces white chocolate, finely
    chopped
¼ cup heavy cream

1 tablespoon vanilla extract
¾ cup confectioners' sugar

Instructions:

Place chopped chocolate in a medium bowl. Place cream in a saucepan and heat over a medium setting until it is just simmering. Remove the cream from the heat and pour it over the chocolate. Let it sit for a minute and then gently stir until it is smooth. (Sometimes white chocolate takes a little longer to melt. If all the chocolate doesn't completely melt, you may want to place the bowl over a pot of hot water.) Stir until all the chocolate is fully melted. When the mixture is smooth, add the vanilla and stir until it is fully incorporated.

Let the ganache cool at room temperature for 30 minutes. Cover the top of the ganache with plastic wrap or parchment cut to fit (the wrap or parchment should sit gently on top of the ganache). Place the bowl in the refrigerator until the ganache is firm (for about 2 hours).

When it is set, scoop out a little more than a teaspoon of the ganache and roll it between the palms of your hands to form a ¾-inch or walnut-sized ball. The truffles don't have to look perfect at this point. Place the balls on parchment paper and return to the refrigerator for about an hour more.

Place the confectioners' sugar in a medium bowl. Take the truffles out of the refrigerator and roll each ball again until it is smooth and round and then immediately roll it in the confectioners' sugar until it is evenly coated. Continue rolling until all the truffles are covered and place them in a single layer in a parchment-lined resealable container.

For best flavor, store truffles at room temperature for up to 4 days or in the refrigerator for up to a week. If you do store them in the refrigerator, make sure to bring the truffles to room temperature before serving.

Bellini White Chocolate Truffles

Created in 1943 by Giuseppe Cipriani, the owner of the famous Harry's Bar in Venice, the Bellini cocktail is a refreshing fusion of peach puree and Champagne. We tried to capture the essence of this sophisticated drink in these truffles. Salute!   **Makes about 20 truffles.**

¼ cup heavy cream
16 ounces white chocolate,
  finely chopped
2 ounces freeze-dried peaches,
  ground to a powder*
3 tablespoons peach schnapps

1 teaspoon Champagne or
  sparkling wine

12 ounces white chocolate,
  finely chopped and divided
Orange sprinkles and sugar pearls
  for decoration
  (optional)

Instructions:

Place cream in a double boiler or a bain marie (heat-resistant bowl over a saucepan ¼ filled with water). Make sure the bottom of the bowl does not touch the water. Heat the cream until it comes to a simmer and then carefully add the 16 ounces of finely chopped white chocolate.

Stir the chocolate/cream mixture until all the chocolate is melted. When the mixture is smooth, remove the bowl from the saucepan and place it on a dish towel. Add the peach powder, peach schnapps, and Champagne and stir gently until the ingredients are thoroughly incorporated.

Let the ganache cool at room temperature for 30 minutes. Cover the top of the ganache with plastic wrap or parchment cut to fit (the wrap or parchment should sit gently on top of the ganache). Place the bowl in the refrigerator until the ganache is firm (for about 2 hours).

When it is set, scoop out a little more than a teaspoon of the ganache and roll between the palms of your hands to form a ¾-inch or walnut-sized ball. The truffles don't have to look perfect at this point. Place the balls on parchment paper and return to the refrigerator for about an hour more. Roll the ganache again, smoothing out any lumps, until the balls are smooth and round.

(recipe continues on next page)

To make the outer coating, take 8 ounces of finely chopped white chocolate and place in a double boiler or bain marie (bowl over a saucepan ¼ full of water). Heat the water over medium-low heat and gently stir the chocolate as it melts. When it is completely melted, remove from the heat and stir in the remaining 4 ounces of finely chopped white chocolate, stirring until smooth. Dip the cool ganache balls in the warm chocolate using the instructions on pages 19–23. Place on a parchment-lined pan and, if desired, sprinkle with orange sprinkles and place a sugar pearl in the center of each truffle for decoration (make sure to add the topping before the chocolate coating dries).

Continue dipping until all the truffles are covered and decorated. Place the truffles in a single layer in a parchment-lined resealable container.

For best flavor, store truffles in the refrigerator for up to a week. Make sure to bring the truffles to room temperature before serving.

* Freeze-dried fruits work well in truffles as they add flavor without adding moisture (which would make the truffles too soft to roll). Freeze-dried peaches can be found in specialty food shops or ordered online.

Cranberry Orange White Chocolate Truffles

These truffles make a splendid autumn treat and a wonderful addition to an elegant Thanksgiving table. The bright fresh flavor of oranges perfectly balances the tartness of cranberries.

Makes about 20 truffles.

(recipe continues on next page)

Cranberry Orange White Chocolate Truffles (continued)

½ cup sweetened dried
  cranberries, finely chopped
2 tablespoons Cointreau
  (or Grand Marnier)
1 tablespoon orange juice
2 teaspoons orange zest
16 ounces white chocolate,
  finely chopped

4 tablespoons heavy cream

12 ounces white chocolate,
  finely chopped and divided
Dried cranberries for decoration
  (optional)

Instructions:

In a small bowl, mix together cranberries, Cointreau, orange juice, and orange zest. Let sit for about 30 minutes.

Place cream in a double boiler or a bain marie (heat-resistant bowl over a saucepan ¼ filled with water). Make sure the bottom of the bowl does not touch the water. Heat the cream until it comes to a simmer and then carefully add the 16 ounces of finely chopped white chocolate.

Stir the chocolate/cream mixture until all the chocolate is melted. When the mixture is smooth, remove the bowl from the saucepan and place it on a dish towel. Add the cranberry mixture and stir gently until the ingredients are thoroughly incorporated.

Let the ganache cool at room temperature for 30 minutes. Cover the top of the ganache with plastic wrap or parchment cut to fit (the wrap or parchment should sit gently on top of the ganache). Place the bowl in the refrigerator until the ganache is firm (for about 2 hours).

When it is set, scoop out a little more than a teaspoon of the ganache and roll between the palms of your hands to form a ¾-inch or walnut-sized ball. The truffles don't have to look perfect at this point. Place the balls on parchment paper and return to the refrigerator for about an hour more. Roll the ganache again, smoothing out any lumps, until the balls are smooth and round.

To make the outer coating, take 8 ounces of finely chopped white chocolate and place in a bain marie. Heat the water over medium-low heat and gently stir the chocolate as it melts. When it is completely melted, remove from the heat and stir in the remaining 4 ounces of finely chopped white chocolate, stirring until smooth. Dip the cool ganache balls in the warm chocolate using the instructions on pages 19–23. Place on a parchment-lined pan and, if desired, gently place dried cranberries on top for decoration (make sure to add the topping before the chocolate coating dries).

Continue dipping until all the truffles are covered and decorated. Place the truffles in a single layer in a parchment-lined resealable container.

For best flavor, store truffles in the refrigerator for up to a week. Make sure to bring the truffles to room temperature before serving.

Dipped in white chocolate and decorated with deep red dried cranberries, these truffles look almost as good as they taste.

Key Lime White Chocolate Truffles

Not as rich in cocoa as its darker counterparts, white chocolate can be a wonderful palette to showcase other flavors, particularly citrus ones. Based on the famous pie invented in Key West, Florida, these tangy treats make a refreshing snack on a hot sunny day.

Makes about 20 truffles.

2 tablespoons vanilla extract
2 tablespoons Key lime juice
1 1/2 tablespoons Key lime zest
16 ounces white chocolate,
 finely chopped
4 tablespoons heavy cream

2/3 cup chopped graham crackers

12 ounces white chocolate, finely
 chopped and divided
Candied lime pieces, sliced thin for
 decoration (optional)

Instructions:

In a small bowl, mix together the vanilla, lime juice, and lime zest. Set aside.

Place cream in a double boiler or a bain marie (heat-resistant bowl over a saucepan 1/4 filled with water). Make sure the bottom of the bowl does not touch the water. Heat the cream until it comes to a simmer and then carefully add the 16 ounces of finely chopped white chocolate.

Stir the chocolate/cream mixture until all the chocolate is melted. When the mixture is smooth, remove the bowl from the saucepan and place it on a dish towel. Add the vanilla/lime mixture and the graham cracker crumbs and stir gently until the ingredients are thoroughly incorporated.

Let the ganache cool at room temperature for 30 minutes. Cover the top of the ganache with plastic wrap or parchment cut to fit (the wrap or parchment should sit gently on top of the ganache). Place the bowl in the refrigerator until the ganache is firm (for about 2 hours).

When it is set, scoop out a little more than a teaspoon of the ganache and roll between the palms of your hands to form a 3/4-inch or walnut-sized ball. The truffles don't have to look perfect at this point. Place the balls on parchment paper and return to the refrigerator for about an hour more. Roll the ganache again, smoothing out any lumps, until the balls are smooth and round.

(recipe continues on next page)

Key Lime White Chocolate Truffles (continued)

To make the outer coating, take 8 ounces of finely chopped white chocolate and place in a bain marie. Heat the water over medium-low heat and gently stir the chocolate as it melts. When it is completely melted, remove from the heat and stir in the remaining 4 ounces of finely chopped white chocolate, stirring until smooth. Dip the cool ganache balls in the warm chocolate using the instructions on pages 19–23. Place on a parchment-lined pan and, if desired, place a piece of candied lime on top of each truffle for decoration (make sure to add the topping before the chocolate coating dries).

Continue dipping until all the truffles are covered and decorated. Place the truffles in a single layer in a parchment-lined resealable container.

For best flavor, store truffles in the refrigerator for up to a week. Make sure to bring the truffles to room temperature before serving.

Key limes are tarter and more aromatic than other limes.
However, they are not always readily available. Be assured,
regular limes will work just as well.

Macadamia Nut Rum White Chocolate Truffles

This is a natural combination. Toasted macadamia nuts, with their salty buttery flavor, help temper the sweetness of the white chocolate. A splash of dark rum adds some depth to the tropical mix.

Makes about 20 truffles.

(recipe continues on next page)

1 cup macadamia nuts,
   chopped and toasted
Pinch of sea salt
2 tablespoons dark rum
16 ounces white chocolate,
   very finely chopped
$^1/_2$ cup heavy cream

12 ounces white chocolate,
   finely chopped and divided
$^1/_4$ cup macadamia nuts, chopped,
   for decoration (optional)

Instructions:

In a small bowl, mix together nuts, sea salt, and dark rum. Set aside.

Place cream in a double boiler or a bain marie (heat-resistant bowl over a saucepan $^1/_4$ filled with water). Make sure the bottom of the bowl does not touch the water. Heat the cream until it comes to a simmer and then carefully add the 16 ounces of finely chopped white chocolate.

Stir the chocolate/cream mixture until all the chocolate is melted. When the mixture is smooth, remove the bowl from the saucepan and place it on a dish towel. Add the macadamia nut mixture and stir gently until the ingredients are thoroughly incorporated.

Let the ganache cool at room temperature for 30 minutes. Cover the top of the ganache with plastic wrap or parchment cut to fit (the wrap or parchment should sit gently on top of the ganache). Place the bowl in the refrigerator until the ganache is firm (for about 2 hours).

When it is set, scoop out a little more than a teaspoon of the ganache and roll between the palms of your hands to form a ¾-inch or walnut-sized ball. The truffles don't have to look perfect at this point. Place the balls on parchment paper and return to the refrigerator for about an hour more. Roll the ganache again, smoothing out any lumps, until the balls are smooth and round.

To make the outer coating, take 8 ounces of finely chopped white chocolate and place in a bain marie. Heat the water over medium-low heat and gently stir the chocolate as it melts. When it is completely melted, remove from the heat and stir in the remaining 4 ounces of finely chopped white chocolate, stirring until smooth. Dip the cool ganache balls in the warm chocolate using the instructions on pages 19–23. Place on a parchment-lined pan and, if desired, add a sprinkling of chopped macadamia nuts to the top of each truffle for decoration (make sure to add the topping before the chocolate coating dries).

Continue dipping until all the truffles are covered and decorated. Place the truffles in a single layer in a parchment-lined resealable container.

For best flavor, store truffles at room temperature for up to 4 days or in the refrigerator for up to a week. If you do store them in the refrigerator, make sure to bring the truffles to room temperature before serving.

Ninety percent of the world's macadamia nuts are grown in Hawaii. They are the hardest nuts to crack, which is probably one reason they are also one of the most expensive.

Peppermint White Chocolate Truffles

Reminiscent of peppermint bark, a longtime holiday favorite, these truffles are even richer and more elegant. Using real mint gives the truffles a natural earthy flavor that is well balanced by the addition of peppermint schnapps and a smidge of peppermint extract. For fun, we've topped the truffles with a bit of peppermint candy.

Makes about 20 truffles.

16 ounces white chocolate, finely chopped

²/₃ cup heavy cream

1 tablespoon fresh mint leaves, finely chopped

2 tablespoons peppermint schnapps

¹/₂ teaspoon peppermint extract

12 ounces white chocolate, finely chopped and divided

Peppermint candies or candy canes, chopped into small pieces (optional)

Instructions:

Place 16 ounces of finely chopped white chocolate in a medium bowl. Place cream and mint leaves in a saucepan and heat over a medium setting until the mixture is just simmering. Remove the cream mixture from the heat and let it sit for 10 minutes. Pour the mixture through a fine-mesh strainer into a bowl. Use a wooden spoon to press down on the mint leaves to impart as much flavor as possible to the cream mixture. Place the strained cream mixture back in the saucepan and reheat it until it is just at a simmer. Pour the cream mixture over the chocolate. Let it sit for a few minutes and then gently stir until it is smooth. Add the peppermint schnapps and the peppermint extract and mix well. (If the mixture appears to separate, you can stir more vigorously or place the ganache in a blender and blend until smooth.)

Let the ganache cool at room temperature for 30 minutes. Cover the top of the ganache with plastic wrap or parchment paper cut to fit (the wrap or parchment should sit gently on top of the ganache). Place the bowl in the refrigerator until the ganache is firm (for about 2 hours.)

When it is set, scoop out a little more than a teaspoon of the ganache and roll between the palms of your hands to form a ³/₄-inch or walnut-sized ball. The truffles don't have to look perfect at this point. Place the balls on parchment paper and return to the refrigerator for about an hour more. Roll the ganache again, smoothing out any lumps, until the balls are smooth and round.

(recipe continues on next page)

Peppermint White Chocolate Truffles *(continued)*

To make the outer coating, take 8 ounces of finely chopped white chocolate and place in a bain marie (bowl over a saucepan ¼ full of water). Heat the water over medium-low heat and gently stir the chocolate as it melts. When it is completely melted, remove from the heat and stir in the remaining 4 ounces of finely chopped white chocolate, stirring until smooth. Dip the cool ganache balls in the warm chocolate using the instructions on pages 19–23. Place on a parchment-lined pan and, if desired, gently place chopped peppermint candies on top for decoration (make sure to add the topping before the chocolate coating dries).

Continue dipping until all the truffles are covered and decorated. Place the truffles in a single layer in a parchment-lined resealable container.

For best flavor, store truffles at room temperature for up to 4 days or in the refrigerator for up to a week. If you do store them in the refrigerator, make sure to bring the truffles to room temperature before serving.

For a little crunch, consider mixing in finely chopped peppermint candies with the schnapps and peppermint extract.

Cognac Spice White Chocolate Truffles

Sophisticated Parisians often conclude an elegant meal with a Café au Cognac, a coffee laced with Cognac and topped with whipped cream. These truffles are reminiscent of this popular after-dinner drink, with the subtle addition of cinnamon and nutmeg spices and chopped almonds. **Makes about 20 truffles.**

(recipe continues on next page)

Cognac Spice White Chocolate Truffles (continued)

3 tablespoons Cognac or brandy
3 teaspoons instant coffee powder
1 teaspoon cinnamon
$^1/_2$ teaspoon freshly grated nutmeg
16 ounces white chocolate,
    very finely chopped
4 tablespoons heavy cream

$^1/_3$ cup almonds, finely chopped

12 ounces milk chocolate, finely
    chopped and divided
White chocolate for drizzle, very
    finely chopped (optional)
Sprinkling of cinnamon (optional)

Instructions:

In a small bowl, mix together Cognac, instant coffee powder, cinnamon, and nutmeg. Set aside.

Place cream in a double boiler or a bain marie (heat-resistant bowl over a saucepan $^1/_4$ full of water). Make sure the bottom of the bowl does not touch the water. Heat the cream until it comes to a simmer and then carefully add the 16 ounces of finely chopped white chocolate.

Stir the chocolate/cream mixture until all the chocolate is melted. When the mixture is smooth, remove the bowl from the saucepan and place it on a dish towel. Add the Cognac mixture and the almonds and stir gently until the ingredients are thoroughly incorporated.

Let the ganache cool at room temperature for 30 minutes. Cover the top of the ganache with plastic wrap or parchment cut to fit (the wrap or parchment should sit gently on top of the ganache). Place the bowl in the refrigerator until the ganache is firm (for about 2 hours).

When it is set, scoop out a little more than a teaspoon of the ganache and roll between the palms of your hands to form a ¾-inch or walnut-sized ball. The truffles don't have to look perfect at this point. Place the balls on parchment paper and return to the refrigerator for about an hour more. Roll the ganache again, smoothing out any lumps, until the balls are smooth and round.

To make the outer coating, take 8 ounces of finely chopped milk chocolate and place in a bain marie. Heat the water over medium-low heat and gently stir the chocolate as it melts. When it is completely melted, remove from the heat and stir in the remaining 4 ounces of finely chopped milk chocolate, stirring until smooth. Dip the cool ganache balls in the warm chocolate using the instructions on pages 19–23. Place on a parchment-lined pan. When the coating has dried, you can decorate the top with white chocolate drizzle and a sprinkle of cinnamon (see page 24–25 for details).

Place the truffles in a single layer in a parchment-lined resealable container.

For best flavor, store truffles in the refrigerator for up to a week. Make sure to bring the truffles to room temperature before serving.

Instead of dipping these truffles, you can roll them in a mixture of confectioners' sugar and cinnamon or chopped almonds.

Orange Grand Marnier White Chocolate Truffles

The blending of orange zest and Grand Marnier lends an intense citrus flavor to white chocolate. Coated in chopped pecans, these truffles are an exquisite indulgence.

Makes about 20 truffles.

Zest of 1 orange
4 tablespoons Grand Marnier
⅔ cup heavy cream

16 ounces white chocolate,
 finely chopped
1 cup pecans, toasted
 and finely chopped

Instructions:

Place the orange zest in a very small bowl with the Grand Marnier. Set aside.

Place cream in a double boiler or a bain marie (heat-resistant bowl over a saucepan ¼ full of water). Make sure the bottom of the bowl does not touch the water. Heat the cream until it comes to a simmer and then carefully add the finely chopped white chocolate.

Stir the chocolate/cream mixture until all the chocolate is melted. When the mixture is smooth, remove the bowl from the saucepan and place it on a dish towel. Add the orange zest/Grand Marnier mixture and stir gently until the ingredients are thoroughly incorporated.

Let the ganache cool at room temperature for 30 minutes. Cover the top of the ganache with plastic wrap or parchment cut to fit (the wrap or parchment should sit gently on top of the ganache). Place the bowl in the refrigerator until the ganache is firm (for about 2 hours).

When it is set, scoop out a little more than a teaspoon of the ganache and roll between the palms of your hands to form a ¾-inch or walnut-sized ball. The truffles don't have to look perfect at this point. Place the balls on parchment paper and return to the refrigerator for about an hour more.

Place the chopped pecans in a medium bowl. Take the truffles out of the refrigerator and roll each ball again until it is smooth and round and then immediately roll it in the chopped pecans until it is evenly coated. Continue rolling until all the truffles are covered and place them in a single layer in a parchment-lined resealable container.

For best flavor, store truffles in the refrigerator for up to a week. Make sure to bring the truffles to room temperature before serving.

Rose Pistachio
White Chocolate Truffles

The delicate floral notes of rose water pair well with mild pistachios to create a romantic confection evocative of the Middle East. Dipped in white chocolate and adorned with candied rose pieces, these bonbons would make a delightful accompaniment to a glass of Champagne.

Makes about 20 truffles.

1/4 cup heavy cream
16 ounces white chocolate,
   finely chopped
2 tablespoons rose water
1 cup pistachios, finely chopped

12 ounces white chocolate,
   finely chopped and divided
Candied rose petals for decoration
   (optional)

Instructions:

Place cream in a double boiler or a bain marie (heat-resistant bowl over a saucepan 1/4 full of water). Make sure the bottom of the bowl does not touch the water. Heat the cream until it comes to a simmer and then carefully add the 16 ounces of finely chopped white chocolate.

Stir the chocolate/cream mixture until all the chocolate is melted. When the mixture is smooth, remove the bowl from the saucepan and place it on a dish towel. Add the rose water and pistachios and stir gently until the ingredients are thoroughly incorporated.

Let the ganache cool at room temperature for 30 minutes. Cover the top of the ganache with plastic wrap or parchment cut to fit (the wrap or parchment should sit gently on top of the ganache). Place the bowl in the refrigerator until the ganache is firm (for about 2 hours).

When it is set, scoop out a little more than a teaspoon of the ganache and roll between the palms of your hands to form a 3/4-inch or walnut-sized ball. The truffles don't have to look perfect at this point. Place the balls on parchment paper and return to the refrigerator for about an hour more. Roll the ganache again, smoothing out any lumps, until the balls are smooth and round.

(recipe continues on next page)

To make the outer coating, take 8 ounces of finely chopped white chocolate and place in a bain marie. Heat the water over medium-low heat and gently stir the chocolate as it melts. When it is completely melted, remove from the heat and stir in the remaining 4 ounces of finely chopped white chocolate, stirring until smooth. Dip the cool ganache balls in the warm chocolate using the instructions on pages 19–23. Place on a parchment-lined pan and, if desired, place a candied rose petal on top of each truffle for decoration (make sure to add the topping before the chocolate coating dries).

Continue dipping until all the truffles are covered and decorated. Place the truffles in a single layer in a parchment-lined resealable container.

For best flavor, store truffles at room temperature for up to 4 days or in the refrigerator for up to a week. If you do store them in the refrigerator, make sure to bring the truffles to room temperature before serving.

Both pistachios and rose water are commonly used in Middle Eastern cuisine, especially in pastries and in candies such as Turkish delight.

Truffle-Inspired Desserts

Chocolate Charlotte

This is a classic French dessert with a twist — the chocolate mousse inside is fashioned from ganache. Featuring Cognac and coffee, this is a sophisticated cake fit for a special occasion.

Makes about 8 servings.

8 ounces bittersweet chocolate, finely chopped
1/3 cup heavy cream
2 teaspoons Cognac

Butter for preparing pan
2 tablespoons Cognac
1 cup strong brewed coffee

1 package of ladyfingers (about 20)

4 large egg whites (kept cold)
Pinch of salt
1/4 cup confectioners' sugar
Crème anglaise (optional)

Instructions:

Place chopped chocolate in a medium bowl. Place cream in a saucepan and heat over a medium setting until it is just simmering. Remove the cream from the heat and pour it over the chocolate. Let it sit for a minute and then vigorously stir until the chocolate is melted. When the mixture is smooth, add the 2 teaspoons of Cognac and stir until it is fully incorporated. Let cool at room temperature.

Meanwhile, butter a round souffle pan (should have a 6-inch diameter and a height of at least 4 inches). In a medium bowl, mix together 2 tablespoons of Cognac with the strong brewed coffee. Dip each ladyfinger briefly in the coffee mix, then arrange them at the bottom of the souffle pan (we place them in a star pattern so that it looks nice when it is unmolded and flipped, but you can arrange them in any configuration as long as they cover the bottom of the pan). Then stand the rest of the ladyfingers around the sides of the pan.

Place the egg whites in a mixing bowl with the pinch of salt. Whip them until soft peaks begin to form. Add confectioners' sugar and continue to beat until the mix is shiny and stiff.

Gently fold 1/3 of the egg white mixture into the cooled chocolate mixture. Then fold in the rest of the egg whites to form a mousse. Pour the mousse into the ladyfinger-lined pan. Cover and refrigerate until the mousse is set, about 4 hours.

To serve, carefully invert the charlotte onto a serving plate and cut into small slices. If desired, serve with crème anglaise (see recipe on page 114). Store in the refrigerator for up to 2 days.

Chocolate Pear Tarts

Filled with luscious dark chocolate ganache, cream, and refreshing pears, these tarts look like they came from a Parisian pâtisserie. You won't believe how simple it is to make something that looks and tastes this good. It looks more daunting than it is — just take one step at a time, and you'll be rewarded with one glorious dessert.

Makes 4 tarts (about 4–8 servings).

For the pâté brisée

1 1/2 cups all-purpose flour
Pinch of salt
1/2 cup unsalted butter, very cold
  and cut into small pieces
2 egg yolks
1/2 teaspoon vanilla extract
1/3 cup confectioners' sugar
2–3 teaspoons water
Butter for preparing pans
Beans or pie weights

For the filling

4 ounces bittersweet chocolate,
  finely chopped
1/4 cup heavy cream

1 15-ounce can of pear halves
  or 4 cooked half pairs
1 egg yolk
1/3 cup heavy cream
Raw sugar to sprinkle on top

Instructions:

To make the pâté brisée, place the flour and salt in a food processor and process until mixed. Add the cold butter pieces and pulse until the mixture looks like coarse meal. In a separate bowl, beat egg yolks with vanilla and confectioners' sugar. Add this to the food processor and pulse until the mixture begins to clump together. Add the water a little at a time, pulsing after each addition until the mixture forms a dough. Gather the dough in a ball, cover it in plastic wrap, and place it in the refrigerator for an hour. (You can prepare the dough in advance and keep it for up to 2 days.)

To make the filling, place chopped chocolate in a medium bowl. Place cream in a saucepan and heat over a medium setting until it is just simmering. Remove the cream from the heat and pour it over the chocolate. Let it sit for a minute and then vigorously stir until it is smooth. Let cool at room temperature.

Butter 4 tart pans. Roll the dough out and cut to fit into each pan. Place the pans in the freezer for 30 minutes.

Preheat the oven to 375°F (190°C). Take the tart pans out of the freezer, place aluminum foil over each one, and fill them with beans or other pie weights. Cook the tarts for 20 minutes, then remove the foil and pie weights and cook for 10 more minutes or until they are golden brown. Let them cool.

(recipe continues on next page)

Divide the ganache among the 4 pans and spread to form a layer at the bottom of each. Take 4 pear halves and place on a cutting board. Make slits starting at the bottom of each pear, leaving the top intact so that all the slices are still attached. Press down on the pear so that it spreads to form a fan shape. Place each half-pear fan on top of the ganache layer of each tart.

In a small bowl, mix the egg yolk with ⅓ cup of heavy cream. Pour 2 or 3 tablespoons of the mixture over each tart and sprinkle raw sugar over them. Place under the broiler (set at low) until the egg mixture sets and the sugar caramelizes. Watch carefully — it happens fast!

The tarts can be stored in the refrigerator for up to 2 days.

These tarts are tastiest if eaten straight from the broiler.
If you wish to make them in advance, you can reheat them
at 250°F (120°C) for about 5 minutes before serving.

Chocolate Ganache Éclairs

This classic French pastry is typically filled with creamy custard and lightly iced with chocolate. The ones shown here are somewhat reversed: filled with milk chocolate ganache with a dollop of whipped cream on the side. **Makes about 8–10 éclairs.**

(recipe continues on next page)

For the éclairs
1 cup water
¾ cup unsalted butter
1 tablespoon confectioners' sugar
Pinch of salt
1 cup all-purpose flour
4 large eggs

For the filling
8 ounces milk chocolate,
  finely chopped
¼ cup heavy cream

Confectioners' sugar for dusting
Whipped cream (optional)

Instructions:
Preheat the oven to 425°F (220°C).

Place the water, butter, sugar, and salt in a saucepan and bring to a boil. Remove pan from the heat and quickly add the flour all at once and mix well. Return the saucepan to the stove and continue to mix until it forms a ball. Place the dough in a bowl and mix it for 1–2 minutes to cool it down. Add eggs one at a time and mix well after each addition. Put batter in a pastry bag (or a resealable zipper storage bag with a small corner cut out) and pipe 2-inch-long éclairs onto a cookie sheet lined with parchment paper. Bake for 8 minutes, then lower temperature to 350°F (175°C) and bake for 15 minutes more or until the éclairs are golden brown. Cool on a rack.

To make the filling, place chopped chocolate in a medium bowl. Place cream in a saucepan and heat over a medium setting until it is just simmering. Remove the cream from the heat and pour it over the chocolate. Let it sit for a minute and then vigorously stir until it is smooth. Let cool at room temperature.

Use a knife to open one side of each éclair (like a book with one side remaining closed). Pipe milk chocolate ganache into the opening of each éclair. Close and dust the top with confectioners' sugar. Serve with a dollop of whipped cream if desired.

The éclairs can be stored in the refrigerator for up to 2 days.

Chocolate Truffle Cookie Sandwiches

Simple to make, this truffle-inspired dessert is a real crowd pleaser. And it's a wonderful way to use up any leftover ganache. The recipe calls for a dark chocolate ganache filling, but any ganache will do. These sophisticated little sandwiches can be served from a tray or, for a more formal presentation, served in a pool of crème anglaise.

Makes 4 cookie sandwiches.

(recipe continues on next page)

4 ounces bittersweet chocolate, finely chopped

¼ cup heavy cream

8 cookies of your choice (medium-sized, with a firm and chewy texture)

½ cup chopped pecans (or other coating of your choice)

Crème anglaise (optional, recipe follows)

For the cookies:

Place chopped chocolate in a medium bowl. Place cream in a saucepan and heat over a medium setting until it is just simmering. Remove the cream from the heat and pour it over the chocolate. Let it sit for a minute and then vigorously stir until it is smooth. Let the ganache cool at room temperature.

When the ganache is firm but still spreadable, place a ½-inch layer on the bottom of one cookie. Cover with the bottom of a second cookie and roll the sides in a bowl of nuts or other coating. If desired, serve with crème anglaise.

The cookies can be stored in the refrigerator for up to 4 days.

For the crème anglaise:

4 egg yolks

½ cup sugar

2 cups milk

1 teaspoon vanilla extract

Instructions:

In a small bowl, beat the egg yolks with the sugar until the mixture is pale. Warm the milk in a saucepan until just simmering. Pour the milk slowly into the egg yolk mixture, whisking thoroughly. Pour the mix back in the saucepan and cook over very low heat, stirring constantly, until the mixture reaches 170°F. The crème anglaise should be thick enough to coat the spoon. Be careful not to boil the mixure or the eggs will start to cook. Remove from the heat and keep stirring for a minute or two. Mix in vanilla. Pour into a bowl, cover the surface with parchment paper, and place in the refrigerator. It should keep for 3 days.

Orange Truffle Mousse in Orange Cups

Served in orange halves, these bright citrus mousse cups make a light and clever dessert. The mousse is made from milk chocolate ganache infused with the juice and zest of an orange.

Makes about 6 servings.

(recipe continues on next page)

7 small oranges (6 reserved for presentation, 1 for zest and juice)
½ teaspoon unflavored gelatin
8 ounces milk chocolate, finely chopped

⅓ cup heavy cream
½ cup heavy cream for whipped cream

Instructions:

Reserve 6 oranges for presentation. Zest 1 orange until you have 1 teaspoon of zest. Squeeze the oranges until you have 2 tablespoons of juice. In a small bowl, mix together the orange zest and juice. Add the gelatin and mix well. Set aside.

Place chopped chocolate in a medium bowl. Place ⅓ cup of heavy cream in a saucepan and heat over a medium setting until it is just simmering. When it comes to a simmer, quickly add the orange mix, stir, and immediately pour it over the chocolate. Let it sit for a minute and then vigorously stir until it is smooth. Let cool at room temperature.

Meanwhile, prepare the orange cups. Wash and dry the 6 oranges and cut off the top third of each. Use a spoon to carefully scoop out the insides of the oranges without damaging the skin. Set orange cups aside.

When the ganache has cooled, whip the remaining ½ cup of cream until stiff and gently fold a third of it into the ganache. Then gently fold in the rest of the whipped cream.

Carefully spoon the mousse into the prepared orange cups. Refrigerate until set, about 4 hours.

Store in the refrigerator. The mousse cups will keep for 2 days.

A decorative slice of orange placed on top of the mousse dresses it up and adds to its elegant appeal.

Creative Packaging

Homemade truffles and other candies make wonderful gifts. And it only takes a little ribbon and some decorative papers to transform a simple gift into something very special.

Following are some ideas on how to creatively package your homemade truffles. Remember, these are just a few suggestions to inspire you and get you started. Use your imagination. The possibilities are endless.

Small Packages for Party and Wedding Favors

Small favor boxes are available at craft stores. Jazz them up with some colorful tissue paper on the inside and ribbon and a few greens on the top for decoration.

Organza bags can also be found in most craft stores. Tied with a simple ribbon, they make elegant packages for your truffles (see photo on opposite page).

Mini planters make unexpected, but fun receptacles for truffles. Cellophane bags keep the truffles neat and can be closed with a colorful ribbon. A little green moss or an ornamental daisy complete the look.

Store-Bought Decorated Boxes

These decorated boxes offer an easy packaging solution. One has an opening on top through which you can glimpse the decorated truffles inside. The other remains closed, guarding its tasty contents.

The elegant gold ribbon that festoons this clear round container brings it to a new level as do its fabulous contents.

Recycled Boxes

Finding a new use for an old box is another good option. Who would ever guess that the box shown here originally held a pen? Tied with a little raffia, the recycled box makes a wonderful peekaboo container for truffles.

Decorated Candy Boxes

A little decorative paper, ribbon, flowers, and buttons have transformed these three plain white candy boxes into something really special.

Double-Duty Gifts

The packages shown here are gifts in themselves, which are made even more special by their homemade contents. Candy dishes are an obvious choice for packaging truffles and are always appreciated by the recipient.

A selection of white truffles look elegant on this mini cake stand.

Double-Duty Gifts

Antique tea cups and saucers make elegant receptables for chocolate truffles. Nestled in the flowered tea cup here are some Espresso Amaretto Dark Chocolate truffles (covered in white chocolate). Tied with a pretty organza ribbon, they are sure to put a smile on the lucky recipient's face.

These Rose Pistachio White Chocolate truffles
look so lovely packaged in this beautiful blue
tea cup. The matching blue ribbon and lavender
flower add a nice touch.

Creative Presentation

Use your imagination. You can use all kinds of things to package your truffles. Here's a mini birdcage filled with truffles. A small bird ornament attached to the top adds to its whimsy.

Pack this handsome planter with a selection of truffles, surround them with soft green moss, and add some raffia for a more rustic gift.

Table of Equivalents

Some of the conversions in these lists have been slightly rounded for measuring convenience.

VOLUME:

U.S.	metric
¼ teaspoon	1.25 milliliters
½ teaspoon	2.5 milliliters
¾ teaspoon	3.75 milliliters
1 teaspoon	5 milliliters
1 tablespoon (3 teaspoons)	15 milliliters
2 tablespoons	30 milliliters
3 tablespoons	45 milliliters
1 fluid ounce (2 tablespoons)	30 milliliters
¼ cup (4 tablespoons)	60 milliliters
⅓ cup	80 milliliters
½ cup	120 milliliters
⅔ cup	160 milliliters
1 cup	240 milliliters
2 cups (1 pint)	480 milliliters
4 cups (1 quart or 32 ounces)	960 milliliters
1 gallon (4 quarts)	3.8 liters

OVEN TEMPERATURE:

fahrenheit	celsius
250	120
275	140
300	150
325	160
350	180
375	190
400	200
425	220
450	230
475	240
500	260

WEIGHT:

U.S.	metric
1 ounce (by weight)	28 grams
1 pound	448 grams
2.2 pounds	1 kilogram

LENGTH:

U.S.	metric
⅛ inch	3 millimeters
¼ inch	6 millimeters
½ inch	12 millimeters
1 inch	2.5 centimeters